CANADA

Troll Associates

CANADA

by Louis Sabin

Illustrated by Allan Eitzen

Troll Associates

Library of Congress Cataloging in Publication Data

Sabin, Louis.
    Canada.

    Summary: A brief introduction to our northern
neighbor, almost as large as the Soviet Union, but
with a population only a tenth as large as that of the
United States.
    1. Canada—Description and travel—Juvenile
literature. [1. Canada] I. Eitzen, Allan, ill.
II. Title.
F1012.S22   1985   971   84-40437
ISBN 0-8167-0302-7 (lib. bdg.)
ISBN 0-8167-0303-5 (pbk.)

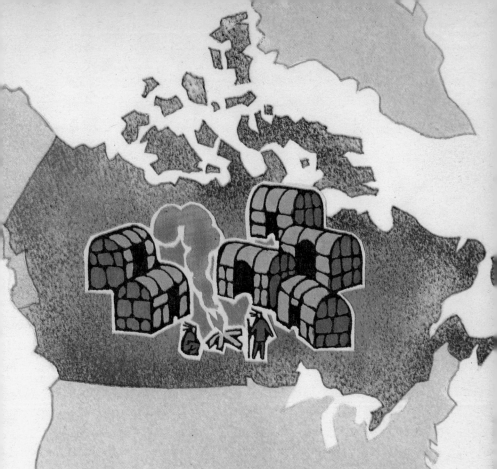

In the language of the Iroquois Indians, the word *Kanada* means "a group of huts" or "a village." It seems strange, then, that the second largest country in the world takes its name from that Indian word. The country of Canada is second only to the Soviet Union in size. Yet its population is only a tenth as large as that of its southern neighbor, the United States.

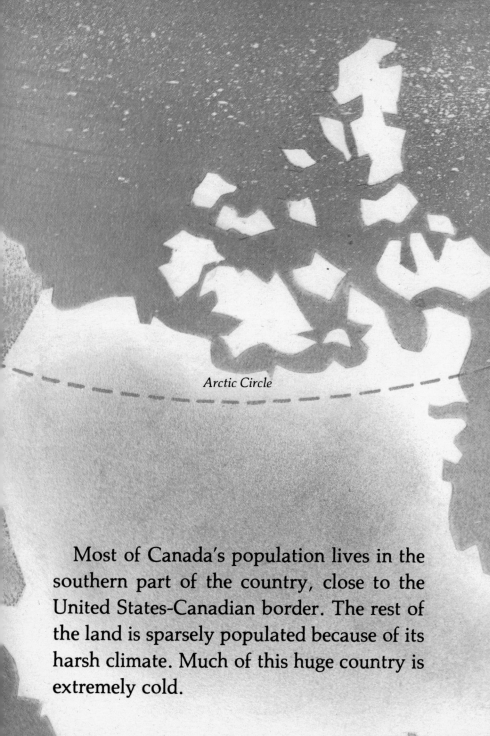

Arctic Circle

Most of Canada's population lives in the southern part of the country, close to the United States-Canadian border. The rest of the land is sparsely populated because of its harsh climate. Much of this huge country is extremely cold.

United States

The northernmost zone of Canada is made up of the Arctic Islands. Like other areas within the Arctic Circle, this part of Canada is gripped by cold all year. The winters are long and dark, with two months of no sun at all. Freezing Arctic winds, a summer too short for crops to grow, and permanently frozen subsoil make Canada's Far North a place where only the hardiest can survive.

The climate is warmer in Canada's western mountain region, or *Cordillera*. The Coast Mountains rise along the Pacific Ocean, forming the western edge of the Cordillera. The Rocky Mountains form the eastern boundary. Between these two mountain ranges lie plateaus, basins, and a long narrow valley called the Rocky Mountain Trench.

The Cordillera has mild winters, particularly along the coast. Warm winds blow in off the warm Pacific Ocean currents. They also bring more rainfall to this region than to any other part of the country. Trees grow well here, and the forests of the west coast are dense and beautiful.

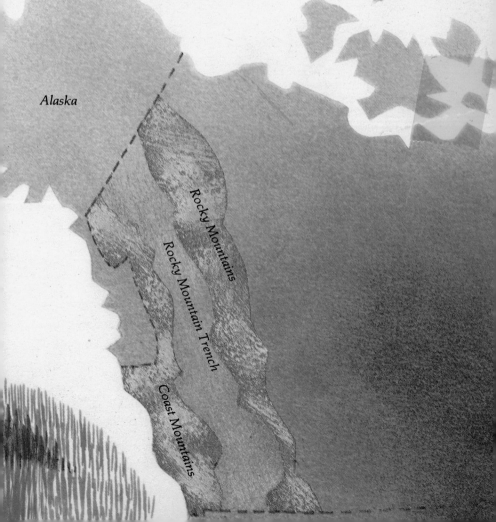

Alaska

Rocky Mountains

Rocky Mountains

Rocky Mountain Trench

Coast Mountains

East of the Cordillera lies the section of Canada known as the western interior plains. Winters here are bitterly cold, with savage winds sweeping down from the Arctic across the broad, open prairies. But summers are pleasant, with warm, dry weather.

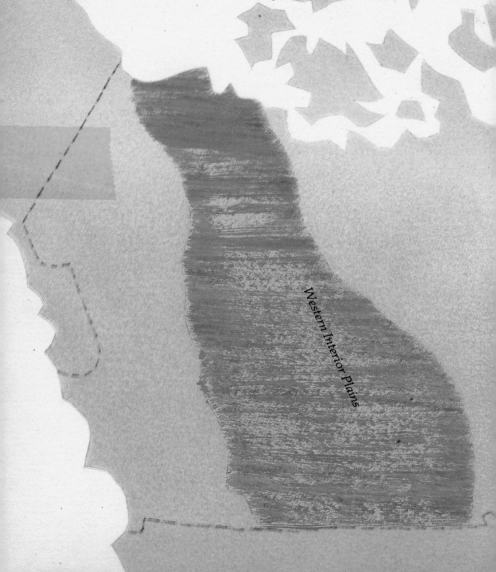

Western Interior Plains

This region contains Canada's richest farm lands. Enormous amounts of wheat, oats, and barley are produced. In addition, many cattle, sheep, and dairy cows graze on the fertile prairie lands. The farms and ranches in this region are vast—sometimes running into thousands of acres.

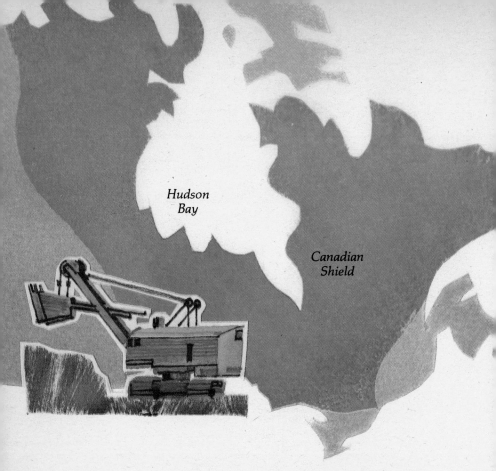

Hudson
Bay

Canadian
Shield

The Canadian Shield lies still further east. It is a horseshoe-shaped region surrounding Hudson Bay. Dotted with lakes, this huge rocky area covers nearly half of Canada. The soil here is poor, but the region is rich in minerals, such as nickel, zinc, and copper. The southern part of the Shield is covered with thick forests, which provide vast amounts of lumber.

Southeastern Canada, also known as the Great Lakes-St. Lawrence lowlands, has cold winters and warm summers. It is the same kind of weather experienced by people living in Michigan, Ohio, Illinois, and New York. More than half the people of Canada make their homes in this region, which includes Canada's two largest cities, Toronto and Montreal.

*Great Lakes-
St. Lawrence Lowlands*

The countryside in the lowlands is fertile and yields large crops of fruit and vegetables. But commerce and industry are the major sources of income and employment in the lowlands.

The Great Lakes and the St. Lawrence River provide easy transportation for goods between this area and the Atlantic Ocean, and between this area and the Mississippi River. This means that Canadian farm products and Canadian manufactured goods can readily be shipped from the lowlands to Europe, South America, or anywhere else in the world.

Great Lakes

St. Lawrence River

Atlantic Ocean

The Appalachian highlands region, in eastern Canada, includes the Maritime Provinces, the island of Newfoundland, and the Gaspé Peninsula of Quebec. The climate in this area is moist most of the year. Winds blowing off the Atlantic Ocean bring summer fog and winter snows and rain. But the Atlantic's warm currents keep this area from getting as cold in winter as inland Canada does.

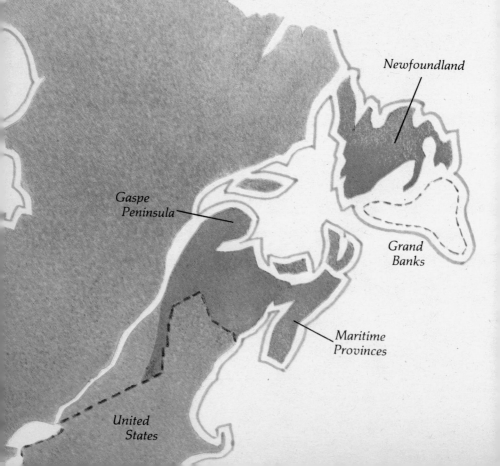

Newfoundland

Gaspe
Peninsula

Grand
Banks

Maritime
Provinces

United
States

The land in this region is similar to the New England section of the United States. There is good farm land, but there is also land where the soil is thin and rocky. A number of harbors dot the coast, because fishing and shipbuilding have long been the major industries here.

Off the coast of Newfoundland lies a section of shallow water called the Grand Banks. This is one of the world's richest fishing grounds. Among the fish caught here are cod, herring, mackerel, haddock, and perch, along with such shellfish as lobsters and crabs.

The nation of Canada is divided into ten provinces and two territories. The provinces are very much like the states of the United States. Each one has a legislature, which is elected by the citizens and which governs affairs within the province.

Yukon
Territory

Northwest
Territories

British
Columbia

Alberta

Saskatchewan

Manitoba

In eastern Canada, the provinces are Nova Scotia, Prince Edward Island, New Brunswick, Newfoundland, Quebec, and Ontario. In western Canada are Manitoba, Saskatchewan, Alberta, British Columbia, and the Yukon and Northwest Territories.

The Yukon and Northwest Territories are mostly run by the federal government of Canada. Like the provinces, the territories have legislatures, but with limited powers. However, the territories hope to reach provincial status someday.

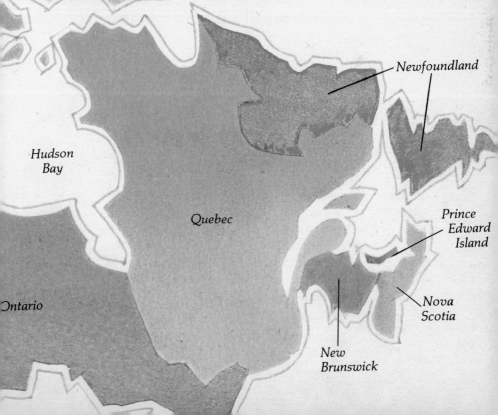

Canada's federal government, located in the capital city of Ottawa, is made up of a two-house parliament. These are called the Senate and the House of Commons. The prime minister is the nation's chief executive. The prime minister is also the leader of the political party that holds a majority of seats in the House of Commons.

Canada is a member of the British Commonwealth. This means that the British monarch is the official head of state. But the title of monarch has no real power attached to it. Canada is a fully independent nation.

Canada was originally settled by people from England and France. Not long after Columbus first reached North America, French explorers set up trading posts and settlements in the Maritime Provinces and along the banks of the St. Lawrence River. These settlements were united in a colony called New France, with Quebec as its capital.

At about the same time, settlers and fur traders from England were coming in large numbers to the New World. Both France and England built forts and claimed vast territorial rights. Their disagreements finally exploded in the French and Indian War. In 1760, the French and their Indian allies were defeated by the British.

The French settlers continued to live in Canada, mostly in the areas north of the Ottawa River. The area south of the Ottawa River was occupied mainly by British settlers. In time, Canada increased in size

Britain

and population until the country's borders stretched from the Atlantic to the Pacific and far up into the Arctic.

Over the years, there has been considerable French influence in eastern Canada. In the province of Quebec, French is the official language. The dominant religion is Catholicism, just as it is in France. The customs, traditions, food, and other aspects of life there remain French in character. The rest of Canada reflects its British heritage and way of life, although both French and English are considered the primary national languages.

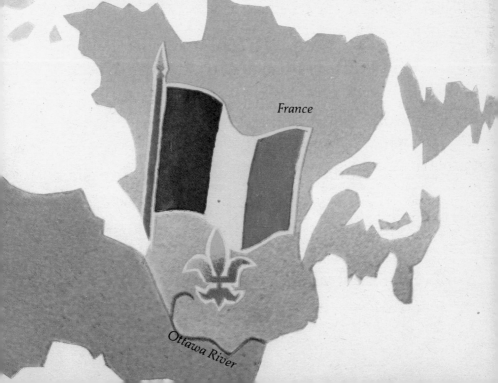

France

Ottawa River

While the French Canadians have been able to keep their traditions, the Indians of Canada have had a much harder time doing so. The ancestors of the Indians and of the Eskimos came to North America from Asia about 25,000 years ago. Some of these early travelers settled in the Polar Region, while others moved south and east throughout North, Central, and South America.

In North America, the Indians formed a number of tribes, including the Cree, Blackfoot, Huron, Sioux, Algonquin, and Iroquois. The various tribes made treaties with the settlers from England and France. Some tribes were allied with the French, others with the English.

But as more and more settlers arrived in Canada, the open land on which the Indians lived was taken from them. Little by little, war and disease reduced the numbers of Canadian Indians. Their land was taken from them and treaties were broken. Some of the Indians left the tribal life entirely, while others went to live on reservations.

The Eskimos of northwest Canada were also affected by the arrival of settlers. The Eskimo way of life was shaken by the Yukon gold rush, fleets of whale and seal hunters, the building of military bases, and the discovery of oil and other minerals.

The newcomers also brought diseases, such as tuberculosis and pneumonia, against which the Eskimos had no resistance. Eskimo culture was also jarred by confusing new machines, laws, ideas, and ways of life that were strange to them.

Today, the Canadian government is working to help the Eskimos, just as it is working to help the Indians of Canada. This is being done with such things as medicine, education, and the opportunity to use their skills to better their standard of living.

For the Eskimos, the Indians, the French-speaking, and the English-speaking people, and for all the immigrants who continue to come to Canada, the future is filled with the promise of greater prosperity and even greater growth.

DATE DUE

APR 21 1998			
APR 20 200			
OCT 9 200			
APR 04			

DEMCO 38-297